IT'S

by

Joyce Willard Teal

Illustrations by

RICHMOND CHAISIRI

Library of Congress Card Catalog Number: 96-90391

ISBN # 1-57502-238-9

Printed in the USA by

Morris Publishing

3212 E. Hwy 30
Kearney, NE 68847
800-650-7888

For Derion Ashley
my love,
my joy,
my inspiration;
my beloved granddaughter

Introduction

Dear Reader,

Zebie, a newborn zebra is born with no stripes. Because zebras are born with and identified by their stripes, as Zebie grows he is unhappy about his stripelessness. Compounding his unhappiness, his playmates, Zill and Zim, tease him about his stripelessness.

Zebie's mother, Zue, and his grandmother, Zulia, have taught Zebie to ignore taunts about his stripelessness. They have taught him that **It's O.K. to be Different.** They have told him that no two zebras are exactly alike, that they all have similarities and they all have differences. Zebie usually feels better after these conversations with his mother and grandmother.

Through conversations with Zim, Zebie learns that royal zebras, King Zavid and Queen Zuth, are bringing their daughter, Princess Zula, to Zee Land. They are bringing her to Zee Land to choose a prince to wed. He asks his grandmother and he learns more about the approaching royal visit.

Zebie, like all of the other male zebras of marriageable age, is invited by the king and queen to a ball being given by them for their daughter. At this ball, Princess Zula is to choose her prince.

Zebie has misgivings about attending the ball. He fears ridicule by the princess when she witnesses his stripelessness. He does not know that the princess has already seen him; he does not know that the princess thinks that he is …

Though Zebie is reluctant, his parents convince him that he must attend the ball. He does and …

Happy **R**eading

Note to Reader

As you read the story, you will notice that in Zee Land, the imaginary land which is the setting for the story, all of the names begin with the letter **Z.** Have fun trying to guess the first letter with which each of the names would begin in the real world in which you live. Share the story with a friend. See which of you can guess the most correctly.

Now think about some of the things that are different and special about yourself. Know that it really is O.K. to be different. Your differences make you the wonderful and very special person who you are. Be happy that you are not just exactly like anybody else. Know that it is our differences that make each of us the unique individuals who we are. And that's pretty amazing!

Autograph page
for
It's O.K. To Be Different

This book belongs to

Donald & Pam

This is a gift from

____

Author's signature

Joyce W. Teal

Date

5/7/00

TABLE OF CONTENTS

CHAPTER 1

Zebie was born one sunny morning in the wilds of Zee Land. Zebie was Zue's first baby, so the fact that he was a baby zebra who was born with no stripes didn't bother her in the least.

When Zebie's dad, Zoe, first saw him he said to Zue, "He's so different from us. He's completely white; he has no stripes."

"That's O.K.," Zue assured him. "He's sure to get his stripes as he grows. Most baby zebras are probably born with no stripes."

"I don't think so," Zoe replied. "When my baby zister was born, I was almost five, and I remember; she had stripes when I first saw her."

"How old was she when you first saw her?" asked Zue. She

rushed on before Zoe could respond. "Maybe she didn't have them when she was first born. Maybe she got them afterward."

"I don't think so. But I didn't see her until the next morning. I was already in bed asleep the night that she was born, so it wasn't until the following morning that I saw her. Maybe you're right. Haven't you ever seen a newborn zebra before?" asked Zoe.

"Never! I've seen babies many times, but none as soon as they were born. So let's not make a big deal of this. He'll probably get his stripes before we know it," Zue says.

"Let's not. Meanwhile, I'll go and let Mom know that Zebie was born early this morning. She's wanted to be a grandzebra for years now. She'll be delighted!" Zoe says as he heads off to find Zulia.

CHAPTER 2

So Zoe goes deep into Zee Land in search of Zulia, his mom. First he meets one of his grazing buddies, Zac. "Zac," he asks, "have you seen Zulia this morning? She's a grandzebra now. My zon, Zebie, was born early this morning and I want to let her know."

"No," said Zac, "but I'll go with you to find her. She's probably somewhere around here eating breakfast."

Now Zoe and Zac together continue the search for Zulia. They gallop along together for about a mile, but they do not find Zulia. Next they encounter Zek. "Zek," asks Zoe, "have you seen Zulia this morning? She's a grandzebra now and I want to let her know. My zon Zebie was born early this morning."

"Yes," replied Zek. "I ate breakfast with her over near that marshy area just east of here. Come along; I'll show you."

So together Zoe, Zac, and Zek go in search of Zulia. As they gallop along Zek says, "Tell us about your zon Zebie. Who does he look like, you or Zue?"

"He looks just like himself," Zoe replies. "He looks just like

Zebie!"

Zac interrupts with, "There's Zulia!" He is pointing with his nose. Zulia is about five-hundred yards ahead. She does not yet see them. "Zulia!" they call simultaneously.

Zulia turns at the sound of her name and sees the three of them galloping toward her. She begins galloping toward them. As the gap narrows she says, "Is everything all right? Has something happened to Zue and the baby?"

"Everything's fine, Mom. Zue had the baby early this morning," Zoe says. "You're a grandzebra now. We named him Zebie in honor of your father. He's beautiful; he's as white as snow."

"Come," says Zulia. "I want to see my first grandzon."

"Can we come too? We also want to see Zebie," Zek says.

"Later," Zoe responds. "My mom gets the honor of this first visit. Alone."

CHAPTER 3

So Zek and Zac head off in the opposite direction as Zoe and Zulia go in search of Zue and Zebie. As Zoe and Zulia gallop along together Zulia says, "Slow down! I'm not as young as you are, you know."

"Mom," says Zoe as he slows, "when I was born, did I already have my stripes?"

"Of course you had stripes. All Zebras are born with their stripes. That's how everyone knows we're zebras," responds Zulia.

Zoe muses over this momentarily, then he says, "Mom, Zebie wasn't born with stripes. He's solid white, and he is a zebra. I know he's a zebra even though he doesn't have his stripes yet. And everyone else will know it too. Come on; you'll see."

As they continue on their journey Zulia is quiet. She is thinking about what Zoe has just told her. She is quite sure that she has never heard of a zebra with no stripes, never, in all of her considerable years. So she says, "You were probably so excited when you saw your firstborn that you just missed his little stripes. Stripes can vary greatly,

you know. Zebie's stripes are probably so light that you just didn't see them in the early morning light. Of course he has stripes!"

"Oh no he doesn't. He's solid white. He's as white as snow," Zoe responds.

There is silence between them as they continue on their way. They hear the chirping of a lone bird; they see the early morning sun shining through the canopy of trees. Finally they reach Zue and Zebie. Zebie is taking his first, faltering steps. He is following a short distance behind Zue. Zue turns and closes the distance between them. She nibbles Zebie on the neck and shoulders, grooming his soft, white skin.

Zulia is dumbfounded. Never before has she seen anything more beautiful. She stares for several minutes thinking that maybe its a zolt or perhaps a giant zabbit. But deep inside she feels a special connection, an attraction, a magnetism. She knows that this is her beloved, long-awaited grandzhild.

"He's beautiful," she mutters, more to herself than to Zoe and Zue who are watching her fearfully. With their keen sense of hearing, they hear her words even though they are muttered. Zoe and Zue look at

one another and smile. If Zulia thinks he's beautiful, then everything must be O.K. Maybe the fact that he has no stripes is not so unusual after all.

4

Two other very young zebras and their mothers are approaching at this time, Zill who was born only two weeks earlier, and Zim who is two months old. They are looking strangely at Zebie. Zim says to Zill, "What is it?"

Zill speculates, "Maybe it's a young zorilla or a baby zorse."

It could be a newborn zog," says Zim. "I don't know what it is, but I know what it isn't, and it isn't a zebra!"

Zue's sharp ears hear this exchange and interrupts it with, "You zhildren stop that right now! He is too a zebra, and a fine one at that. Just look at him. He's only hours old and already he's walking. What does it matter that he doesn't look exactly like you? Does that mean that he doesn't have feelings like you do? How would you two like it if one of the older zids said that the two of you were not zebras?"

Zill and Zim hang their heads and trot away without comment. Before long they encounter Zarolyn, the brain of the herd. "Zarolyn," says Zim, "Mrs. Zue has a new baby, but he doesn't look like her, and he doesn't look like Mr. Zoe either. He's solid white; he has no stripes."

Zarolyn muses over this for several seconds, then she says disdainfully, “Perhaps he’s zalbino,” and trots off before either Zill or Zim can ask her to explain.

“Zalbino? I wonder what that means?” muses Zill aloud. “I’m going to ask my mom,” says Zim, and off he goes in search of his mother.

CHAPTER 5

Zebie is a wonderful zhild and his family loves him very much. He is the delight of his granzy's heart, and at times she is almost able to forget that he is a zebra with no stripes. Some of Zebie's playmates sometimes make fun of him. He usually ignores them and continues his playing. Occasionally Zebie feels sad and unhappy because of the taunts. His mom and granzy have told him to ignore them, and most of the time he is able to do so, but the taunts still hurt. Today one of his playmates begins to chant, ZEBIE LOST HIS STRIPES, Soon two others join in. Zebie runs home crying.

His mother sees him approaching and trots out to meet him. "What's the matter, Zebie?" she asks. "Are you O.K.?"

"My friends tease me. They say I lost my stripes. Mom, why don't I have stripes like Zim and Zill and you and Dad? Why do I have to be so different?" Zebie asks tearfully.

"Zebie," says Zue, "it's O.K. to be different. No one is really like anyone else anyhow. We all have similarities and we all have differences. Look in the brook," she says as she motions for him to follow her to the small section of Lake Zee closest to the two of them. Isn't your face shaped just like mine? Don't our eyes and ears look a lot alike?"

Zebie examines himself and his mom's face carefully. He silently stares into the crystal clear waters of Lake Zee. He can see himself and his mom's reflections. "We do look alike, don't we? If I had stripes, or if you had no stripes, we'd be just like twins. Wouldn't we?" he says.

"Not exactly. And you wouldn't want to be exactly like me, or exactly like anyone else either, for that matter. I want to look just like me, and you should want to look just like you. There's absolutely nothing wrong with the way you look," Zue tells him.

"But Mom, I'm supposed to be a zebra. Zebras are known to have stripes. I don't have any stripes. So what am I?"

"Zebie, you're a zebra; you know you're a zebra, and so does anyone else who sees you. It is not stripes that make us zebras. Stripes are just one of our characteristics. There are many others that are of far greater importance. No one knows why we have stripes anyhow. We certainly don't need stripes to function. Can't you run and play just as well as any of your striped playmates? Don't you eat and sleep just like the rest of us? Don't you bleed when you get a cut? Don't you have feelings just like the rest of us?"

"Yes, but my friends are teasing me."

"Zebie, if they were really your friends, they would not tease you about your stripelessness. They know you're sensitive about that. Real friends don't intentionally hurt one another. Real friendship doesn't hurt, it heals. Real friendship feels good and is supportive."

Zebie does not respond this time to Zue's words, but he is thinking about them as he returns to where his playmates are. Several of them who are grazing nearby look up as he approaches.

"Hi Zebie. Where'd you disappear to? We were looking for you," Zim says.

"I went home for a while. I wasn't feeling so good. But I'm O.K. now," Zebie tells him.

CHAPTER 6

"Zebie, the king and queen are coming to Zee Land. They are bringing their zaughter, Princess Zula, to choose a prince. Have you heard? Everyone is talking about it. It is rumored that they will be here exactly two weeks from today," Zim says breathlessly. "I'm so excited! I've never seen a king or queen before."

"Why is she coming here to choose a prince? There're no princes here," Zebie responds.

"Sure there are. Any of us can be a prince. All we have to do is marry a princess, then we're a prince. I hope Princess Zula chooses me. She can choose whomever she wants to be her prince," Zim tells Zebie.

"Then I hope she chooses me," Zebie says.

"You! Why would she choose you?" Zim asks as he laughs at the idea.

"Well, you said she could choose whomever she wants. Maybe she'll choose me just because she wants to choose me. You did say it's her choice, didn't you?" asks Zebie.

"Yes, I said it. And it is her choice. But I'll bet she won't choose you," Zim says.

"Probably not," says Zebie. "And she probably won't choose you either. I'm not getting my hopes up, and I suggest you don't buy your wedding tux just yet either."

Later that evening, as Zebie is preparing for bed, he says to Zue, "Mom, is it true that the king and queen are coming to Zee Land and that they're bringing Princess Zula to choose her prince? Zim says there's going to be a grand ball and everything."

"Yes, it's true. Once before, a long time ago, a king and queen came here. It happened so long ago that I can't even remember it. My mom told me about it."

"Did that king and queen zebra also have a princess zebra, and did they bring her here with them to choose a prince?" Zebie asked.

"As a matter of fact, they had a zon. They brought their prince here to choose his princess. In fact, that prince and his princess are now the very same king and queen zebras who are bringing their princess here to choose her prince," Zue tells him.

"Well, did he choose a princess from here in Zee Land?"

"He did. And according to my mother, she was one of the local zirls, the zaughter of one of my grandmother's friends. There was a grand ball, right here in Zee Land. My mother said that she got an invitation to it, embossed in gold. Ask your granzy about it. She knows a lot more about it than I do," Zue tells him.

CHAPTER 7

"Granzy, Mom told me that you knew about a king and a queen, royal zebras, who came to Zee Land once a long time ago. Tell me about it," says Zebie.

"Well, it was a long, long time ago. But I haven't forgotten. The king and queen brought their zon to Zee Land to choose a princess to wed. There was a grand ball. All of the eligible young zadies were invited. You should have seen them. I didn't go to the ball myself. I was too young, but I saw all of the pretty zirls as they passed my clearing on their way to the ball. Everyzody was so sure that the prince would choose Zandria. She was very beautiful. But apparently beauty was not all that the prince desired. He didn't choose Zandria. He chose Zophia instead. Zophia wasn't nearly as pretty as Zandria, although she was a pretty zirl. But it was widely known that while Zandria was confident of her beauty, and quite vain because of it, Zophia didn't believe herself to be pretty. In fact, as I recall, rumor had it that Zophia had intended to miss the ball, altogether, believing herself to have no chance to be chosen by the prince. But her mother wouldn't hear of it. The king and queen had asked that every eligible zirl in Zee Land attend the ball and" . . . Zebie interrupts with "Granzy, what does 'eligible' mean?"

She explains that eligible means capable or legally qualified for something, and that in this context it means all of the zirls who were of marriageable age. Then she continues.

"As I was saying, the king and queen had asked that every zirl of marriageable age attend the ball. In those days, no one dared defy a king or queen. Anyhow, Zophia did go to the ball. Everyzody at the ball said that the prince had danced with more than fifty zirls before Zophia's turn came, and that she went shyly into his arms. They said she wouldn't even look into his eyes, and that he tilted her head upward by placing a royal thumb underneath her chin. It was rumored that from that moment on they were inseparable."

"What's inseparable, Granzy?" asks Zebie.

"It means that they stayed together. Nobody could separate them, ever. She became his princess. There was a magnificient wedding with twenty brideszaids, held right at the royal palace. She became his princess and they lived happily ever afterwards. In fact, that very same prince and princess are now the king and queen, the very same who are bringing their princess here to choose her prince. But enough of this king and queen talk. I'm getting hungry. Are you ready to eat?"

CHAPTER 8

Days passed and everywhere in Zee Land the talk was of the approaching ball. Mom zebras began taking extra care, grooming their zons beautiful, striped coats several times daily, and teaching them additional grooming techniques to assure their readiness for the ball. Zebie watched enviously as well-groomed, striped zebras trotted, almost prancing, with the realization that they looked sleek and beautiful.

"Come," Zue said to Zebie one morning. I must groom your wonderful, white coat and show you how to care for it. You must be ready for the ball. It's only a few days away, you know. You must be ready for the ball this Saturday night."

As Zebie approached Zue and submitted to her grooming nibbles and strokes, all he could think of was how different his coat was from the other eligible zons who would be in attendance at the ball, and about how the princess would laugh when she saw him.

"She may even have me thrown out as an imposter. She may not even recognize me as a zebra, Mom. Maybe I shouldn't even attend the ball."

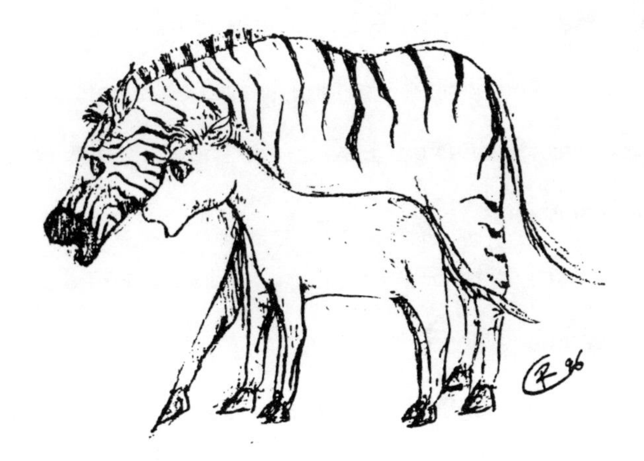

"You stop that kind of talk this instant!" Zue responds. "Of course you should go. Didn't the king and queen send you a gold-embossed invitation requesting the honor of your presence, just as they sent to all of the other eligible zons?"

"Yes, but they haven't seen me. If they had, maybe I wouldn't have gotten an invitation."

"Zebie, that's nonsense. The king and queen probably have not seen any of the others either, but they want every eligible young zan in Zee Land at the ball. That includes you. So no more talk about your not being there. And besides, the king and queen arrived in Zee Land with their princess weeks ago. How do you know that they haven't seen you? They could have."

Zebie makes no response because he doesn't know, but while the king and queen have indeed not seen him, Princess Zula has seen him. While looking out of her third-floor window, three days after their arrival in Zee Land, she spotted what she described to the queen and king as "The most beautiful, white coat I've ever seen." She went on to say, "And I'm sure a zebra was wearing it. I'm almost certain a zebra had on the alluring, white, sleek coat. It was of the purest white. It looked satiny and furry both at the same time. It's hard for me to describe. I've never seen anything like it. But I could tell by the angle of its ears and the tilt of its head that it was indeed a zebra, and a very unique one too."

CHAPTER 9

"Why didn't you take a closer look, princess? You should have sent one of your royal zervants to fetch him for you. I'm sure he would've been honored to meet a beautiful princess such as yourself," Queen Zuth says.

"I wanted a closer look, but I was so stunned by the beauty of it that by the time I was able to think clearly, he had trotted off in the opposite direction. Since then, I've watched daily from the very same window, but I've not seen him again. I've seen lots of other zebras, all with beautiful, striped coats, but none as beautiful as the solid, white one that glistened in the sun. Do you think I'll ever see him again, Queen Mother?" asked Princess Zula.

"Of course you will if you desire to do so. If he's of an age he'll be at the ball, your ball. And you can get as close a look as you'd like. Is he of an eligible age?" asked Queen Zuth.

"I'm sure of it. He's at least as old as I am from what I could see," the princess says.

"Then he'll be at the ball. It is decreed in all of Zee Land."

"I know what I'll do, I'll ask Zaul, the royal sculptor, to sculpt a bust of him. I'll describe him as best I can," Princess Zula tells her mother.

CHAPTER 10

Preparations for the ball are now complete. The royal Zee Land Palace, which has stood unoccupied for decades, with only a skeletal staff to attend it, was readied as soon as it was known that King Zavid and Queen Zuth would be bringing Princess Zula to Zee Land to choose her prince.

The ballroom is at its most resplendent. Thousands of lights glitter throughout. Strains of exquisite music fill the ballroom. Fountains tinkle in basins of snow-white marble. The fragrance of a thousand wildflowers perfume the air. The young, eligible, male zebras are gorgeously robed, radiant in their striped coats, but for one: Zebie. Zebie's coat is even more radiant, of the purest white. Zue has groomed his coat twice daily for days now, and even Zebie, when no one was around to observe him, sneaked peeks at his reflection when he had occasion to go near a section of the sparkling waters of Lake Zee.

As was the custom in Zee Land whenever there was a royal ball, each zebra mom would present her eligible zon to the king and queen first, and then to their princess, or each zebra dad would present his zaughter first to the king and queen, and then to the prince. Following the introduction, the presented zon or zaughter would dance with the prince or princess. Afterwards, he or she would be free to dance with other guests. If the prince or princess desired a second dance with any invited guest, a knight was sent to the guest with a note requesting that the guest approach the prince or princess and ask for the honor of a second waltz.

The presentations continued for more than an hour. The princess has now danced with every eligible zon, except one: Zebie. Very discreetly, as each zon was being presented and all attention was focused on the presentation, Zebie would trade places with the next zebra to his right. Zue would be forced to do the same in her line if she wished to remain directly across from her zon in the line of zebra moms facing the zons. She has tried, repeatedly, to catch Zebie's eye and to admonish him silently to stop moving to delay his introduction to the princess. But he has refused to look at her. He knows what her thoughts are.

Delay is no longer possible. Haltingly, Zebie steps forward. Zue too moves forward to take her zon's arm. She says loudly and clearly, "May I present my zon, Zebie."

While Zebie's presentation is being made to the king and queen, there is an audible intake of breath which is heard throughout the ballroom. All heads turn in the direction of Princess Zula from which this gasp has come. She is staring at Zebie, wide-eyed and wonderingly. As Zue moves slightly to present Zebie to Princess Zula, she is wondering what this gasp means. Princess Zula touches her nose to Zebie's nose, something she has done to none of the other zons with whom she has danced. Zue wonders too what this means. But she is no longer fearing that her beloved Zebie will be rejected. She can sense acceptance, and maybe even adoration, in the eyes of Princess Zula.

"I saw you," the princess whispers to Zebie as they waltz around the ballroom. "I saw you when I looked out of my bedroom window almost a week ago. Every day after that I watched for you, but you did not return. Fearing that you were lost to me forever, I asked my royal

sculptor to sculpt a bust in your image. I've never seen skin as beautiful as yours. You have no stripes in your beautiful, lustrous coat." All of this is whispered as Zebie and Princess Zula waltz around the ballroom.

With each of the other zons, Princess Zula waltzed only one rotation around the ballroom, but she and Zebie are now beginning their third rotation. All of the other zebras are beginning to whisper among themselves. What does this mean? They wonder. Has Zebie already been chosen to become Princess Zula's prince? It couldn't be, could it?

Zarolyn, the brain, says to Zim as they take a turn around the floor, "Isn't it obvious that the princess is quite taken with Zebie? She can't take her eyes off him."

"No such thing is obvious! She's just being courteous," responds Zim. "In a few minutes she'll begin sending her knight with requests to some of us for a second dance, you'll see." Zarolyn makes no response to this, but her superior intelligence has allowed her to understand what Zim has yet to comprehend: **the princess has made**

her choice, and it is ZEBIE.

And so it is that Zebie, and all of Zee Land, learns that it's O.K. to be different. Being different doesn't mean being better or being worse. That, of course, is determined by individual aspiration and effort. But differences are determined by nature, some of them at any rate.

Zebie has learned to accept that he is different, and that his differentness does not make him any less of a zebra than the different patterns of stripes observed throughout Zee Land make the striped zebras less than what they are. Zebie has learned a lesson that we can all learn: **it is our differences that make each of us uniquely ourselves!**

INTERESTING FACTS ABOUT REAL ZEBRAS

1. Zebras are striped members of the horse family.
2. Zebras live in herds in the deserts and grasslands of eastern and southern Africa.
3. There are three species of zebras.
4. Each of the three species of zebras has a distinctive stripe pattern.
5. Much like fingerprints in humans, no individual zebra's stripes are identical to those of another zebra.
6. Experiments have shown that from birth zebras are attracted to objects with stripes.
7. Zebras with abnormal stripe patterns are usually not allowed in the herd and seldom survive.
8. Zebras spend 60 to 80 percent of their time eating.
9. Zebras protect themselves from predators by keeping together in herds.
10. A zebra's night vision is as good as an owl's.
11. Zebras can run at speeds of up to 40 miles (65 kilometers) per hour.
12. Zebras may live up to 22 years in the wild.
13. A zebra herd may range in size from a few individuals to several hundred.
14. Females become sexually mature at age three and may reproduce throughout the rest of their lives.
15. The female zebra carries a single young, called a foal, inside her body for about a year before giving birth.

From Information finder © 1995 World Book, Inc.

CELEBRATE DIVERSITY

Celebrate diversity! Being different

Is just fine.

How would the wine connoisseur feel if

There were only one wine?

Celebrate diversity! Add to the

Melting pot.

Ask people kindly about their differences,

And you could learn a lot.

Celebrate diversity! Be glad that

We're not all twins.

When we celebrate diversity,

Everyone wins!

Everybody's heritage is important.

Everybody's special, don't you see?

We can all listen and learn; love and speak,

So let's **celebrate diversity!**

Glossary of Terms

Absolutely (10): definitely; without a doubt

Admonish (10): to warn; to reporve gently

Alluring (17): attractive, enticing

Aspiration (22): ambition: yearning

Assure (16): make certain of

Audible (20): capable of being heard

Bridesmaids (6): young, unmarried female who is a bride's attendant

Bust (18): head, shoulders, and breast of someone represented in sculpture

Canopy (6): covering

Chant (9): a monotonous song

Characteristics (10): traits; identifying marks

Comprehend (22): understand

Considerable (5): more than a few; many

Courteous (21): polite

Decade (19): ten consecutive years

Decreed (18): officially ordered; judicial decision

Defy (15): resist openly

Discreetly (20): so as not to attract attention

Disdainfully (22): haughty or indignant

Dumbfounded (6): in stunned amazement

Eligible (14): legally qualified

Embossed (13): raised in relief from the surface

Exquisite (19): refined; choice; excellent

Faltering (6): in a weak and trembling manner; tentative

Fetch (18): to go after and bring

Function (10): to perform a function or duty

Gorgeously (19): splendid; inclined to magnificence

Imposter (16): one who falsely pretends

Inseparable (15): impossible to separate

Intentionally (10): done with purpose; intended

Lustrous (21): glowing; having a sheen

Magnetism (5): an attraction

Magnificient (15): grandeur of appearance; splendor

Marriageable (15): able to get married; eligible

Momentarily (5): in a moment; shortly

Obvious (21): clear; easy to understand

Occasionally (9): once in a while; sometimes

Presentations (20): introductions

Radiant (19): brilliant; splendid

Realization (16): real belief

Rejected (21): to discard as useless

Rotation (20): regular succession

Rumored (11): popular report; frequently said

Sculpt (18): to carve or cut stone or other material into an image

Sculptor (18): one who cuts or carves materials, such as stone, into images

Sensitive (10): easily affected; easily hurt

Skeletal staff (19): a minimal group of workers

Speculates (7): makes a guess

Superior (22): higher than others

Supportive (11): upholds; helpful

Taunts (9): insulting language which is meant to injure

Techniques (10): artful ways

Tilt (17): angle; slant

Unique (17): single in its kind; unequaled

Unoccupied (19): empty

Waltz (20): a dance for couples